Hadar

CW00850846

DIARY OF A YOUNG BLACK KING
BLACK HISTORY:
Real Life Superheroes

To Amari

Enjoy this Journey through black history

HSankofa

Diary of a Young Black King: Black History - Real Life Superheroes
by Hadar Sankofa
First publication 2022. With the services of book publishers Sun Cycle Publishers.
email: suncyclepublishers@mail.com
tel: 044 (0)7599504680

SunCyclebooks

To Grandad

DIARY

of a Young Black King:

BLACK HISTORY

REAL LIFE
SUPERHEROES

BY HADAR SANKOFA
AGED 10

Hi, I'm HADAR.
I wrote a diary every month on
what I learnt about Black History.
I discovered a lot of cool and
interesting things about some
amazing and heroic people.
To me they are Real Life
Superheroes.

Me ↗

Enjoy!
Hadar Sankofa

BLACK HISTORY
The Roots of Civilization

BLACK HISTORY 24/7/365

All human populations on Earth today can trace their ancestry back to Africa. There's no evidence you can use to trace the human record back to any other location.

My Avatar ↗

All human Y-DNA has been traced to a single male who scientists call The African Adam, who lived 142,000 years ago, as stated in the Journal of Human Genetics. The lineage of all modern humans can be traced back to a single African woman, known to scientists as The Mitochondrial Eve, who lived about 200,000 years ago.

THE BLACK PANTHER KING

Dear Diary,
Black Panther is one of my favourite films.
Chadwick Boseman was an African-American actor.
He acted as The Marvel Superhero T'Challa in the movie
Black Panther. The film is one of the highest money
-making movies of all time. It made more than 1 billion
dollars around the world!

Chadwick sadly died shortly after of cancer. British rapper Stormzy wrote a song for Chadwick, called SUPERHEROES. You can watch the music video on YouTube. Chadwick will be forever remembered as a real-life Superhero. He did many inspirational things.

He spoke up against stereotypical roles and gave hope to other cancer patients like him. He was unstoppable even when he was unwell.

Superheroes by Stormzy

R.I.P Chadwick Boseman

THE BLACK PANTHER PARTY

Today I learnt about The Black Panther Party, originally called the Black Panther Party for Self-Defence. They were formed in the 1960s to protect families in the community.

The Black Panthers were known for their
Free Breakfast Program that helped poor and hungry
school children, as well as having a Black Panther
ambulance, health program and charities that gave
free clothes and food to poor people.

The Black Panthers also defended against injustice,
which got them into a lot of problems because they
believed in defending themselves against any kind
of injustice.

Bobby Seale and Huey P. Newton started the Black
Panthers on October 15, 1966, in Oakland, California.

They helped a lot of people and solved problems in the community as civil rights leaders.

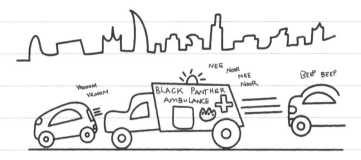

They became positive role models and real-life Superheroes in the neighbourhoods they served.

THE BERBERS

I did some research on Morocco, North Africa, before I travelled there on Holiday. Here's my story... A long time ago, there was a tribe in Africa called The Berbers.

The Berbers are Nomads of the Sahara Desert. Nomads are people who travel around in mobile homes and don't stay in one place for long periods of time.

Sand Dunes

The Sahara Desert in North Africa is almost the same size as Europe.

Sahara desert

Europe

Berbers wear head wraps called turbans and travel on camels instead of horses.

Turban head wrap →

Desert Camel

In the cities, some Moroccan people live in RIADS which are homes with inside gardens. Also, in the dry Sahara Desert, there is an interesting thing called an OASIS.

Riad houses

In the middle of the hot desert, you may be lucky to find an Oasis. It has freshwater, green plants and provides rest, shade, food and water for Nomads.

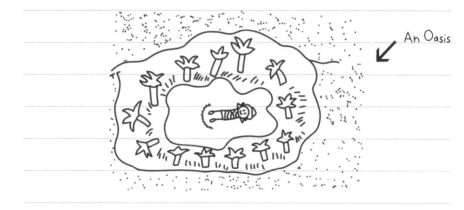

An Oasis

THE SMARTPHONE INVENTOR
Jesse Eugene Russell

Many people think the invention of the smartphone
was by big technology companies like iPhone or Android,
but in fact, the first digital cell phone was invented by
an African-American man named Jesse Eugene Russell.
Jesse was working as an engineer, and in 1988,
he created the concept for the wireless digital phone.

THE GREAT CARTHAGINIANS OF AFRICA
General Hannibal

Guess what I learnt today... I learnt about a great soldier: his name, Hannibal of Carthage. Carthage was a city in Tunisia, North Africa. The Romans tried to take General Hannibal's country.

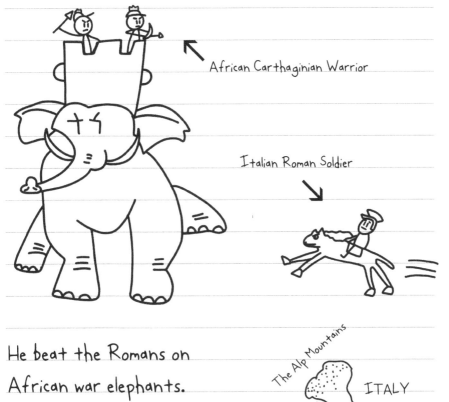

African Carthaginian Warrior

Italian Roman Soldier

He beat the Romans on
African war elephants.
The tiny horses of the Romans
were no match for them.
Hannibal was a very smart thinker.
With his army, he rode over the cold
Alp mountains to Italy to surprise
and beat the Roman army.

The Alp Mountains

ITALY

Rome

Carthage
(Modern day Tunisia)

AFRICA

THE PHONE and LIGHT BULB INVENTOR
Lewis Latimer

Mr Latimer was born in 1848 in America. He is one of the most important black inventors.

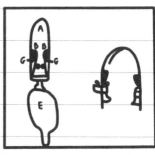

Electric lamp patent by Lewis Latimer.

An inventor is someone who creates new things. He patented many inventions. A patent is a certificate that proves who made an invention. In history, Thomas Edison is famous for inventing the light bulb.

But his light bulb only lasted for a few hours at a time. Lewis Latimer improved the light bulb, which made it last much, much longer. Lewis Latimer wrote the first-ever book about electric lights, it was called Incandescent Electric Lighting.

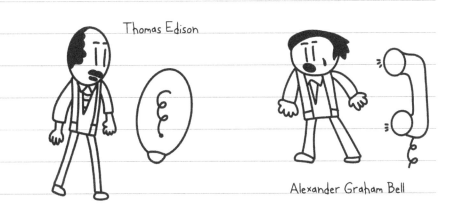

Thomas Edison

Alexander Graham Bell

Lewis Latimer didn't only improve the light bulb. He also helped inventor Alexander Graham Bell improve the telephone in 1876. If it wasn't for Lewis Latimer, we might not have had smartphones today.

APRIL

My Short Story About...
THE RICHEST MAN (EVER)

Dear Diary,
A few centuries ago in Africa, there was a great
and a kind King called MANSA MUSA.

He was the richest man to ever live. Richer than any man today. In modern money, he would be worth more than 400 Billion dollars!

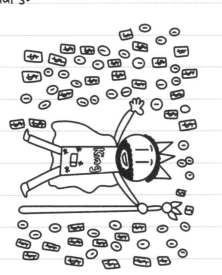

He owned half the world's supply of salt and gold.

MANSA MUSA ruled at least 400 cities. He was a very kind man. He made sure anyone he saw was always given gold. He ruled a large part of Sudan in Africa.

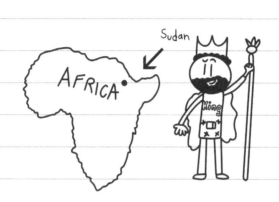

After his death, he couldn't rule anymore.

THE INVENTOR OF THE TRAFFIC LIGHT

Garrett Morgan

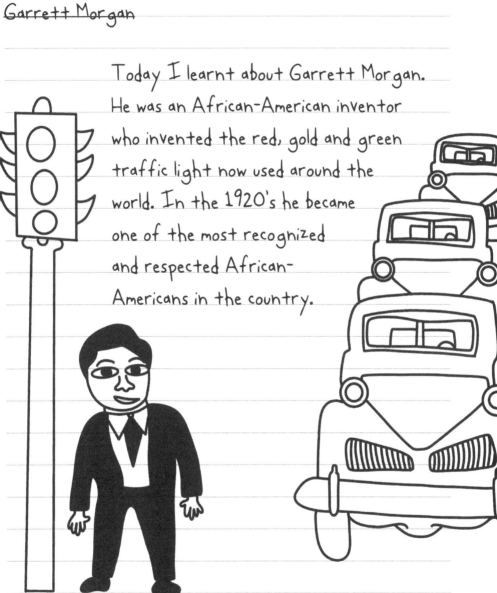

Today I learnt about Garrett Morgan. He was an African-American inventor who invented the red, gold and green traffic light now used around the world. In the 1920's he became one of the most recognized and respected African-Americans in the country.

THE BRAVE ETHIOPIAN GENERAL (AGED 15)
Jagama Kello

Dear Diary,

This is amazing! At age 15, a brave Ethiopian boy who became a general, known for his big afro hair, helped free his North African people from the Italian army.

Jagama

His older brother

His name is Jagama Kello. He was only a boy when he fought for his freedom with his older brother and an army of brave Ethiopian men and women to defend their country in 1935.

Empress
Menen Asfaw

Emperor
Haile Selassie

Ethiopia is a country in North Africa, is also famous for its royal emperor called Haile Selassie and his queen, empress Menen Asfaw. The Ethiopian Emperor king is part of a great family called the Solomonic dynasty, whose ancestors can be found in the Bible as King Solomon and the queen of Sheba.

THE GREAT POET RAPPER
Tupac Amaru Shakur

I listened to some of Tupac's music and decided to do some more research on him. Tupac Amaru Shakur was an American rapper, poet and actor. He rapped about the problems faced by African-Americans and people around the world.

His mother, Afeni Shakur, was a civil rights activist. She was a member of the Black Panther Party, and so was Tupac's father.

Tupac held the Guinness World Record for the highest-selling rap/hip hop artist.

THE GREAT LEADER
Malcolm X

Today I researched Malcolm X. He was an African-
American minister, inspirational speaker, and human
rights activist in the 1960's.
Human rights mean things
like having the right to
freedom as a human being,
the right to education and
the right to be treated
fairly. Malcolm's father
was a church minister and
activist who followed the
teachings of Marcus Garvey.
His mother was a secretary
for the Marcus Garvey Movement.
You can find Malcolm's videos on YouTube.
His speeches still inspire people today. Such as
his famous saying, "By Any Means Necessary".

THE GARVEY MOVEMENT
Marcus Garvey

Marcus Garvey was a great leader of the 1900s. He encouraged Black people to be proud of their African heritage. His goal was to start a new Black country in Africa. He bought a fleet of ships called The Black Star Line to bring African-Americans back to the home of their ancestors - Africa.

Before social media was around, Mr Garvey had millions of followers all over the world. He was known as The Black Moses.

Mr Garvey was an inspiration for many black leaders that came after him, including Martin Luther King Jnr., Elijah Muhammad, Malcolm X and The Black Panther Party.

THE HOLISTIC HEALERS

Some doctors work in hospitals, other doctors heal people using natural herbs, fruits, vegetables and plants. Dr Sebi, Dr Afrika and Dr Valentine are natural holistic healers.

Dr. Sebi   Dr. Llaila Afrika   Dr. Phil Valentine

Holistic means not just healing one part of the human body but the whole body. The three doctors are heroes in keeping the community healthy naturally.

THE SUPERHEROES OF HAITI

In the 1800s, the British, American, French and Spanish armies were chased away by the brave free men of Haiti. Haiti is a country in the Caribbean.
A few brave men by the names of Toussaint Louverture, Jean-Jacques Dessalines, Henry Christophe, and Boukman were enslaved workers who stood up for their human rights and fought for their freedom. They were superhero freedom fighters. Their superpowers: Bravery, courage and protectors.

Emperor
Dessalines

President
Toussaint L'Ouverture

King
Henry Christophe

Boukman Dutty
The Jamaican Maroon

THE BLACK CHEDDAR MAN OF ENGLAND

The oldest skeleton found in Britain was a black man. Scientists named him Cheddar Man. He lived 10,000 years ago. Modern Europeans came much later.

Studies by Harvard University in 2015 proved that European, Indian, and Chinese people came from African ancestors. They proved this by studying fossils. CHEDDAR MAN is the oldest skeleton to ever be found in Britain. Scientists at London's Natural History Museum discovered that he was a black man.

African people were the first people on Earth.
It's a scientific fact! All other humans came from
the ancestry of African people.

Cheddar Man's bones were found in a town called
'Cheddar Gore' in Somerset, UK, which is why scientists
call him Cheddar Man! You can still see his skeleton at
The Natural History Museum – Human Evolution Gallery,
in London.

THE KING - MLK

Martin Luther King Jr., sometimes called MLK for short, was a civil rights activist in the 1950s and 60s.

He led non-violent protests in the USA where African-Americans were treated badly back then. MLK was brave enough to do something about it. The first courageous thing MLK became famous for was defending an elder lady called Rosa Parks, who was arrested for refusing to give up her seat on a bus because of the colour of her skin.

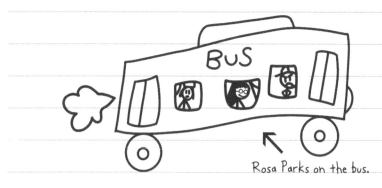

Rosa Parks on the bus.

In 1963 MLK helped organize the famous March on Washington, the capital city of America. To protest for a change in the laws.

It was here that he gave his speech called "I have a dream", which became one of the most famous speeches in history.

March on Washington.

THE 1ST PHARAOH KING OF EGYPT

Menes was the first Pharaoh of Egypt, he ruled over 5000 years ago. This started the beginning of one

of the greatest civilizations that we can still see today, such as the great pyramids of Giza and stone temples in Karnak, Egypt, Africa.

He is known for uniting, and bringing the different parts of Egypt together and building it into one of the world's greatest empires.

He is also known as The Scorpion King.

THE AFRICAN OLMECS OF MEXICO

The African Olmecs lived 3000 years ago in Mexico, South America. They created large stone pyramids, writing and number systems, and even had a calendar system!

We know of them today because they left huge stone heads carved to look like their faces.

The statues are still around today and are called The Olmec colossal heads, which were carved out of huge rocks. They are the height of two men. These stone statues are now in museums in Mexico.

THE PLANT GENIUS
George Washington Carver

Mr Washington Carver was an African American teacher and scientist born in 1860. He loved growing and farming. He was a botanist, which is someone who works with plants. He is known for his scientific work with peanuts and sweet potatoes!

Washington won worldwide respect for his work as a scientist. With his laboratory work, he developed more than 300 inventions from peanuts such as PEANUT: milk, plastics, paints, dyes, cosmetics, medicinal oils, soap, ink, wood stains.

He also invented 118 products from SWEET POTATOES such as molasses, postage stamp glue, flour, vinegar and synthetic rubber and even a type of gasoline.

Mr Washington Carver's efforts won him many honours and improved life throughout the entire American South.

MY SUPERHERO GRANDAD

And finally,
Dear Diary.

This book is dedicated to
my special Superhero,
My grandad. Who became
an ancestor in 2021.

His name was Otis John,
and he was from Guyana,
South America. Known
by the nickname Prince.
He taught me so many
things that I will always
remember.

One day when I'm a grown man,
I will be just like you.

Love you always Grandad.
You will always be My Superhero.

Lightning Source UK Ltd.
Milton Keynes UK
UKHW052139150422
401624UK00001B/1